Cheerleading

TEAM SPIRIT
CHEERLEADING

GETTING THE EDGE: CONDITIONING, INJURIES, AND LEGAL & ILLICIT DRUGS

Baseball and Softball

Basketball

Cheerleading

Extreme Sports

Football

Gymnastics

Hockey

Lacrosse

Martial Arts

Soccer

Track & Field

Volleyball

Weightlifting

Wrestling

Team Spirit CHEERLEADI

Cheerleading

by Gabrielle Vanderhoof

Mason Crest Publishers

Copyright © 2011 by Mason Crest Publishers. All rights reserved. No part of this publication may be reproduced or transmitted in any form or by any means, electronic or mechanical, including photocopying, recording, taping, or any information storage and retrieval system, without permission from the publisher.

MASON CREST PUBLISHERS INC.
370 Reed Road
Broomall, Pennsylvania 19008
(866)MCP-BOOK (toll free)
www.masoncrest.com

First Printing
9 8 7 6 5 4 3 2 1

Library of Congress Cataloging-in-Publication Data

Vanderhoof, Gabrielle.
  Cheerleading / Gabrielle Vanderhoof.
     p. cm. — (Getting the edge: conditioning, injuries, and legal & illicit drugs)
  Includes bibliographical references and index.
  ISBN 978-1-4222-1732-0   ISBN (series) 978-1-4222-1728-3
  1. Cheerleading—Juvenile literature. 2. Cheerleading—Training—Juvenile literature. I. Title.
  LB3635.V36 2010
  791.6'4—dc22
                                   2010010052

Produced by Harding House Publishing Service, Inc.
www.hardinghousepages.com
Interior Design by MK Bassett-Harvey.
Cover Design by Torque Advertising + Design.
Printed in the USA by Bang Printing.

The creators of this book have made every effort to provide accurate information, but it should not be used as a substitute for the help and services of trained professionals.

Contents

team spirit
CHEERLEADING

Introduction

GETTING THE EDGE: CONDITIONING, INJURIES, AND LEGAL & ILLICIT DRUGS is a fourteen-volume series written for young people who are interested in learning about various sports and how to participate in them safely. Each volume examines the history of the sport and the rules of play; it also acts as a guide for prevention and treatment of injuries, and includes instruction on stretching, warming up, and strength training, all of which can help players avoid the most common musculoskeletal injuries. Each volume also includes tips on healthy nutrition for athletes, as well as information on the risks of using performance-enhancing drugs or other illegal substances. GETTING THE EDGE offers ways for readers to healthily and legally improve their performance and gain more enjoyment from playing sports. Young athletes will find these volumes informative and helpful in their pursuit of excellence.

Sports medicine professionals assigned to a sport with which they are not familiar can also benefit from this series. For example, a football athletic trainer may need to provide medical care for a local gymnastics meet. Although the emergency medical principles and action plan would remain the same, the athletic trainer could provide better care for the gymnasts after reading a simple overview of the principles of gymnastics in GETTING THE EDGE.

Although these books offer an overview, they are not intended to be comprehensive in the recognition and management of sports injuries. They should not replace the professional advice of a trainer, doctor, or nutritionist. The text helps the reader appreciate and gain awareness of the sport's history, standard training techniques, common injuries, dietary guidelines, and the dangers of using drugs to gain an advantage. Reference material and directed readings are provided for those who want to delve further into these subjects.

Written in a direct and easily accessible style, GETTING THE EDGE is an enjoyable series that will help young people learn about sports and sports medicine.

—*Susan Saliba, Ph.D., National Athletic Trainers' Association Education Council*

1
Overview of Cheerleading

Understanding the Words

Choreography *is the composition and arrangement of dances.*

A **mentor** *is a trusted counselor or guide who advises.*

Perseverance *is the ability to stick with something and not give up.*

Anatomy *is the study of the structures of organisms.*

Physiology *is a branch of biology dealing with the process of life and living organisms.*

Physical therapy *is treatment that uses exercise, equipment, and massage.*

The History of Cheerleading

Cheerleading—the pom-poms, the outfits, and the yells—is a sport so closely linked with high school and college as to be almost inseparable. Many a teenage girl has dreamed of being a cheerleader. Not that this sport is just for women; many college teams are mixed, and, what's more, the first cheerleaders were men.

Sometime in the 1870s, Thomas Peebler gathered six men on the sidelines of a Princeton university football game and led them in an organized yell before the student body. According to records, the yell went as follows: "Ray, Ray, Ray! Tiger, Tiger, Tiger! Sis, Sis, Sis! Boom, Boom, Boom! Aaaaaah! Princeton, Princeton, Princeton!"

In 1884, Peebler shared this yell with the University of Minnesota. The student body there quickly adopted it, and on November 2, 1898, a young man by the name of Johnny Campbell got so excited by the yell that he left his seat and went to stand in front of the crowd, jumping and waving his arms in excitement.

The first cheerleaders were men who stood in front of the crowd at football games and led cheers. This image shows a cheerleader at a 1939 football game between Duke University and North Carolina.

Later, the university introduced the first organized cheerleaders and the first official "fight song." The first cheerleader fraternity, known as Gamma Sigma, was formed there in 1900.

Cheerleaders have used megaphones since the early twentieth century. These World War II military cheerleaders are rousing the crowd during a New Year's Day football game in Florence, Italy.

Cheerleading equipment became standardized during the early twentieth century. At first, team spirits had been roused by drums and noisemakers, such as the horns and whistles used for New Year's Eve parties. The megaphone and the pom-pom now replaced these. Megaphones, which had been used sporadically in cheerleading since the sport's beginning, became a popular staple of cheerleading squads. Pom-poms were introduced in the 1930s, made originally from paper. The pom-poms of today, made from vinyl, were introduced in 1965 by Fred Gastoff and later adopted by the International Cheerleading Foundation, now known as the World Cheerleading Association.

In the 1920s, women began to take an active interest in cheerleading. At the same time, the components of cheerleading began to change. No longer content with just leading yells, cheerleaders of the 1930s and '40s incorporated gymnastics and tumbling into their cheer routines. Cheerleading continued to evolve throughout the 1940s and '50s. For example, regulations and standards for cheers and stunts were put into place, and more and more women were taking part. In 1948, Laurence "Hurkie" Hurkimer organized the

Today female cheerleaders are commonplace, but in the beginning cheerleaders were only men. Women started to become involved in the 1920s—these women are some of the first female cheerleaders at the University of Wisconsin in the mid-1950s.

Famous Cheerleaders

Many famous people, including politicians, actors and sing-
ers, have also been cheerleaders. Some of the names might
surprise you:

- Madonna
- Steve Martin
- George W. Bush
- Luke Perry
- Jamie Lee Curtis
- Ronald Reagan
- Kirk Douglas
- Franklin D. Roosevelt

- Dwight D. Eisenhower
- Cybil Shepherd
- Sally Field
- Jimmy Stewart
- Teri Hatcher
- Meryl Streep
- Samuel L. Jackson
- Raquel Welch

first cheerleading camp at Sam Houstan University in Huntsville, Texas. Fifty-
two girls attended, and the camp was considered quite a success. Hurkimer
went on to found the National Cheerleading Association, and he also created
several slogans, ribbons, and buttons that cheerleading teams sold to raise
both student spirit and much-needed funds.

Cheerleading became increasingly important at schools and colleges
throughout the United States. By the 1950s, other colleges were conduct-
ing cheerleading workshops to teach basic cheerleading skills. In 1967, the
first ranking of the Top Ten College Cheer Squads was released, and the
International Cheerleading Foundation (ICF) held the first Cheerleaders All
America award ceremony. That same year, the Baltimore Colts football team
organized the first professional cheerleading squad.

Fun Facts

- At the University of Kentucky, the average cheerleader is about 5 feet (1.5 m) tall and weighs 97 pounds (44 kg).
- About 98 percent of all female cheerleaders are former gymnasts, compared to just 20 percent of male cheerleaders.
- Lila McCann, country music star, performed cheerleading routines for Elizabeth II, Queen of England.
- There are at least four million cheerleaders in thirty-one countries.
- Twelve percent of cheerleaders are five to thirteen years old.
- Twelve percent of cheerleaders are also dancers.
- Eighty-three percent of all cheerleaders have a B grade point average or better.
- Sixty-two percent of cheerleaders are involved in a second sport.
- Eighty percent of schools in the United States have cheerleading squads.
- The most popular sport for cheerleading is football.

(Source: cheerleading.about.com)

In 1972, a Texan, Tex Schramm, raised professional cheerleading to a new level. Traditionally, women stood on the sidelines yelling cheers. Now Schramm had the idea of forming the cheerleaders into a squad of dancers, who would serve to complement and support the actual football team. Auditions were held and training began. The "new and improved" Dallas Cowboys cheerleaders were introduced in the 1972–1973 N.F.L. season, and a new form of entertainment was born.

The Dallas Cowboys cheerleaders were the first cheerleaders to incorporate dance as a major part of their routines.

Prior to the 1970s, cheerleaders had primarily supported a school's football and basketball teams. During the 1970s, however, cheerleaders began to support a wide variety of other sports, including wrestling, track, swimming, and volleyball. At some schools, the same cheer squad supported all these teams; larger schools formed separate squads for each sport.

In 1978, with the support of the ICF, CBS-TV broadcast the first nationally televised Collegiate Cheerleading Championships. In 1976, the Dallas Cowboys Cheerleaders performed at Super Bowl X, thereby starting a trend, both among other professional teams and among high school and university squads, for an emphasis on dance routines in cheerleading.

Today, cheerleaders around the world do dance routines and lead crowds in cheering for sports from baseball to volleyball. These Polish girls are cheering for a local rugby team.

Today, cheerleading is a recognized sport around the world. Even though it is mostly identified with American football, the concept of cheerleading has expanded to many other sports. Brazil, China, and Latvia have professional volleyball cheerleading; New Zealand and South Africa women cheer on their rugby teams; and Venezuela has cheerleaders for baseball.

There are competitions at the middle school, high school, and college levels, and universal standards and guidelines have been established. Training courses for cheerleading coaches and sponsors span the United States. Cheerleading has certainly come a long way since Johnny Campbell jumped out of his seat and rushed to the front of the student body!

Careers in Cheerleading

Cheerleading is a highly competitive sport that takes a great deal of drive and determination, especially if you want to become a professional cheerleader. Most of those who become professional cheerleaders have been working at it since they were very young (the average being three years old). And while there are many male cheerleaders on college and university teams, there are no male professional cheerleaders as of yet.

PROFESSIONAL CHEERLEADING

The track to become a professional cheerleader often begins in high school. Many professional cheerleaders were on their high school and college squads and participated in dance lessons since they were very young. They have a desire to entertain and are not shy about being in front of a crowd. In fact, training in dance—whether ballet, jazz, tap, or hip-hop—is an integral part of becoming a professional cheerleader. Today, many organizations specialize in training people to become cheerleaders, providing training in modern dance, choreography, and cheerleading techniques.

Becoming a professional cheerleader is much like becoming a professional in any sport. To be successful, you must be determined, and you need

Tryout Do's and Don'ts

- **DO** study the current members of your school's cheerleading squad. The more you look and act like a member of the team, the more likely your chances are of being selected as one.

- **DO** be yourself. These first two points may seem like a contradiction, but while it is a good idea to show that you are willing to be a team player, it is also important that you stay true to yourself and your character. In other words, **DON'T** compromise your personality in order to conform to an ideal.

- **DO** practice cheerleading moves and dance routines at home. Practicing in front of a mirror will help you perfect your moves—you won't always look to an audience the way you see yourself in your mind, so it's important to see yourself from others' point of view. Practicing in front of family members or friends will help you get used to performing in front of crowds.

to build up experience. Try out for your school's cheerleading team if you have not already done so. If you fail to make it the first year, try not to be discouraged. Think of it as an opportunity to further develop your skills. Take dance lessons and find people who either have been or are cheerleaders and ask them to be a mentor for you. By the time the next tryouts roll around, you will be ready to give it your all.

- **DON'T** be a poor loser. If you don't make the team this time, do not bad-mouth the coach, the judging committee, or those who did make the team. Sometimes, people quit or get kicked off the team, and if word gets out that you are a poor loser, you are unlikely to be asked to try out for the now-vacant spot, or make the team next year.
- **DON'T** ever give up.

If you didn't make the team this year, ask the cheerleading coach what you can do to improve. Take dance and/or gymnastics classes. Try out as many times as you possibly can.

If you make a mistake during tryouts, just take a deep breath and start again. Your persistence, determination, and confidence will be noticed and may even help to earn you a spot on the team.

After the high school level, you can pursue cheerleading at your college or university. This is usually the next step on the path to becoming a professional cheerleader. Professional sports teams and organizations all over the world have cheerleading squads, for football, basketball, soccer, even wrestling.

Other organizations offer cheerleading scholarships, such as the World Cheerleading Associations (WCA), Christian Cheerleaders of America, and the U.S.A. Cheerleading Federation. Talk to your school's guidance counselor, visit the career center at your library, or talk to cheerleading coaches at the colleges you are considering in order to find out what cheerleading scholarships are available; over three hundred U.S. colleges offer them. Some of the most well-respected schools for cheerleading include the University of Kentucky, the University of Arizona, the University of Louisville, the College of Charleston (South Carolina), and Duke University, among many others.

Cheerleading competitions are available at middle school, high school and college levels. This high school team spent over a year preparing a two-and-a-half minute routine combining tumbling, stunts and dance.

2009 National Cheerleading Association (NCA) Collegiate National Championships Results

1. University of Louisville (KY)
2. Oklahoma State University (OK)
3. Texas Tech University (TX)
4. North Carolina State University (NC)
5. Purdue University (IN)
6. Virginia Tech (VA)
7. University of Akron (OH)
8. University of South Carolina (SC)
9. University at Buffalo (NY)

These were the top nine teams in Division IA competition. However, there are many categories to compete in at the National Championships: Division I, Division II, Small Coed, All Girl, Junior College, Coed Intermediate, All Girl Intermediate, Dance Divisions, Dance Innovative Choreography, Group Stunt, and Partner Stunt.

Tryouts are the most typical way to get on a professional cheerleading squad, just as it is in high school or college. Again, you may have to go through a lot of tryouts before you finally secure a spot on a professional team, but with hard work, perseverance, and a positive attitude, you very well may achieve your goal.

PROFESSIONAL CHEERLEADING COACHING

The average age of most professional cheerleaders is twenty-three. Cheerleading is a sport that demands a lot from the body, which means that your career as a professional will usually be over by the time you are in your mid-thirties, if not earlier. This does not mean that your career in the sport has to end. Many people who have had successful careers as cheerleaders go on to become successful cheerleading coaches—and they are not limited to only professional teams. Coaches are needed for a wide range of ages, from middle school all the way up through college.

Again, professional cheerleading coaches arrive at this job largely by way of passion, devotion, and a determination to serve the sport of cheerleading. If you decide in high school or college that you want to be a coach, consider taking courses in **anatomy**, **physiology**, physical education, dance, and **physical therapy**. In addition, consider getting a teaching certificate with a concentration in physical education, as many cheerleading coaches in schools and university are also teachers or professors.

Being a professional cheerleading coach is a serious endeavor, and the sport demands a lot from the squad members and coaches alike. According to cheerleading coach Linda Rae Chappell, there are several key components to being a successful coach:

- All coaches should have a cheerleading philosophy upon which all decisions as a coach are made.

- All coaches should have a firm passion for cheerleading.

- The goal of every cheerleading coach should be to help cheerleaders develop physically, psychologically, socially, and academically.

- Coaches should try to be the best role model possible for their cheerleaders.

There are many options when it comes to coaching cheerleading, and you can narrow your focus by examining your own interests and passions; for example, if you love children, consider coaching a small elementary squad. Or, if you are a great gymnast, perhaps you can work toward coaching a high-level competitive team. Don't limit yourself to just one team or one goal. Explore what is available and what you love most.

Professional cheerleading is not the only career option for post-college cheerleaders—coaching young cheerleaders can be a challenging and rewarding choice. This head cheerleading coach is showing members of her squad the proper technique for a cradle dismount.

2
Mental Preparation

Understanding the Words

Hydrated *means to have enough water.*

Rehearsed *means practiced, went over (either mentally or verbally). You can rehearse something by doing it—but you can also rehearse it by thinking about it step by step, or by describing it step by step.*

Inspiration *is the act of raising emotions and thoughts to a high level of activity by stimulating and encouraging.*

Preparation is the best way to prevent any sports injury. This is no different for cheerleading, a sport that combines gymnastics, dance, and tumbling. The sport takes place on a variety of surfaces, including asphalt, polished wood, and grass. It's important to be warmed up and prepared for whatever comes your way.

You probably already know that the muscles of your body should be warmed up with stretches and other exercises—but have you every given any thought to mental preparation? For a long time, many people in the Western world believed that the mind and the body were two completely separate things. However, we are now coming to understand more and more about the connections between the body and the mind. In fact, they are not separate at all; what you think and feel correlates directly to your physical state. In turn, how your body feels affects the types of messages sent to the brain, affecting your mental state.

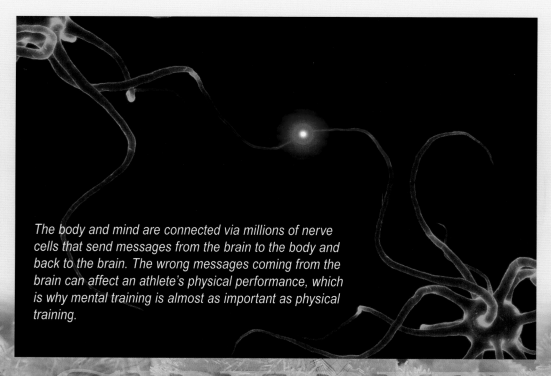

The body and mind are connected via millions of nerve cells that send messages from the brain to the body and back to the brain. The wrong messages coming from the brain can affect an athlete's physical performance, which is why mental training is almost as important as physical training.

Take advantage of the link between the body and mind when you are preparing yourself for cheerleading. If you are injured or too tired to continue, don't ignore your feelings; take a break. If you feel thirsty, be sure to stay hydrated to avoid problems later on. Taking hints from your body can improve your performance drastically, so don't ignore what it's telling you.

As a cheerleader, your concentration, awareness, and discipline are just as important as your skills and technique on the floor. Mental preparation that builds these qualities can take many forms, including visualization, goal setting, and attitude, developing a sense of humor, and positive thinking.

Visualizations

Visualization in terms of sports preparation means you see yourself in your mind's eye performing an activity correctly and without injury. Suppose, for example, you are concerned about a new cheerleading routine you need to master. Close your eyes and picture yourself in your head performing the routine perfectly. When it comes time to actually do the routine, the fact that you have rehearsed it mentally so many times will give you the confidence to perform without making mistakes.

Goals

While practicing or competing in cheerleading (or any sport, really) set goals for yourself. Personal goals, goals you have as a cheerleading team, or a combination of both can help you stay focused and motivated. Think about what it is you want to achieve as a cheerleader, and keep in mind that no goal is too big or too small. Your goals could include mastering a difficult jump, learning a new dance routine, or making a particular cheerleading team.

Whatever your goals are, write them down. The act of writing down your goals will make them more concrete in your mind and can also serve as a constant reminder of what you are trying to achieve. Put your list of goals in a place where you will look at them at least a couple times a day, such as your bathroom mirror or your locker at school.

Inspiration

It can be hard at times to stick to our goals, especially when it seems like you are a long way from achieving them or you are stuck in one place. Combat these feelings by looking for inspiration. When you feel inspired, you have an

Young cheerleaders can find some of their inspiration from role models—older cheerleaders who set positive examples and provide goals for which to strive.

What Are People Saying About Cheerleading?

In recent years cheerleading has evolved from a school-spirit activity into an activity demanding high levels of gymnastics skill and athleticism.
—Brenda Shields, author

Cheerleading is not what it used to be. It's no longer standing on the sidelines looking cute in a skirt.
—Erin Brookes, former cheerleader and safety coach

It appeals to everyone. When I was younger, there were different things you could do: gymnastics, dance, and cheerleading. Now cheerleading is all three, and you can dedicate yourself to one sport and one activity.
—Whitney Hommel, cheerleading coach

I love cheerleading because of the adrenaline rush right before a competition.
—Latoya Holland, former cheerleader and cheerleading coach.

I think cheerleading is something every little girl thinks about doing, and now, with so many places to cheer, more have an opportunity to do so.
—Danielle Muckleroy, former cheerleader and personal trainer

Inspiration

If you can dream it, you can do it.
—Walt Disney

Your talent is God's gift to you. What you do with it is your gift back to God.
—Leo Buscaglia

Obstacles don't have to stop you. If you run into a wall, don't turn around and give up. Figure out how to climb it, go through it, or work around it.
—Michael Jackson

A happy person is not a person in a certain set of circumstances, but rather a person with a certain set of attitudes.
—Hugh Downs

You've got to say, "I think that if I keep working at this and want it badly enough I can have it." It's called perseverance.
—Lee J. Iacocca

attitude in which you believe you can do anything you set your mind to—and you can! Inspire yourself by finding quotations or sayings you find meaningful, watch performances by an accomplished cheerleader you admire, or even have a pep talk with your coach or fellow teammate. Also, write down inspirational sayings that inspire you and leave them where you can read the quotes often, near your written-down goals. By reminding yourself what your goals are, why you have them, and visualizing yourself achieving those things, you will go a long way toward mastering them.

Affirmations

In addition to writing down your goals and providing yourself with inspiration, affirmations are a good way to get yourself mentally prepared for cheerleading. These are positively worded statements that reflect a desire or goal. For example, you could repeat this sentence to yourself over and over: "I am doing my absolute best and I am *good*!"

Let's say this is your first year trying out for the cheerleading squad and you are understandably nervous. There are cheers to memorize, routines to learn, and you have to come up with your own routine and perform it in front of many people—possibly even the whole school!

Rather than panicking, however, and feeling like there is no way you can possibly do it, try this: close your eyes and visualize yourself performing the cheer or routine correctly. Let your imagination run free. Imagine that everyone is clapping and cheering for you because you did such a great job. Picture yourself in the cheerleading uniform at the big football game, leading the crowds in cheers of victory. Repeat affirmations to yourself, such as, "I am a member of the cheerleading squad," or, "I am performing my routines perfectly."

Notice that these affirmations are worded in the present. In other words, you should say them as if you are doing them right now, as opposed to

*I am enthusiastic—
I can be a winner*

Positive affirmations can be a good way to keep the proper mental attitude. Combining affirmative statements with inspiring images on affirmation cards that are read each day is one way to practice this mental exercise.

sometime in the future. By phrasing your affirmations this way, the goals are made more concrete and real in your mind. There's an old adage that says, "Fake it till you make it." By pretending you are a successful cheer-leader and imagining yourself as such, it may not be long before your dream becomes a reality!

Don't Forget to Exercise Your Funny Bone

All the affirmations, visualizations, inspirational sayings, and other positive thinking you can conjure up may not help when you suffer a setback or a disappointment. Disappointment is only natural, especially if you don't make the squad you'd hoped or you make a mistake in front of the crowd, but when these things happen, keep them in perspective and maintain a sense of humor. Things could always be worse.

One cheerleader shared this story on the website cheerleading.about. com:

It was a week before nationals, and we were practicing at the well-known GymTyme. There was a section of the cheer where we had to put up liberty, power press, and heel stretch. We were making our transitions to our stunts when my root foot got caught in one of my left foot's show laces. I tripped horribly, falling to my face! (It was a padded floor so it was no big deal.) One of my fellow cheerleaders tried to save me from that embarrassing fall, but all she did was pull my pants down . . . and my boxers! We were also sharing the floor

Superstitions, like those surrounding the spirit stick can aid in an athlete's mental preparation process. However, a superstition can negatively impact an athlete if she places too much belief in the superstition over her own talents.

with three-time national N.C.A. champions. I pulled my clothing back up fast, but it wasn't quick enough to spare me the embarrassment of showing myself . . . everyone in the gym that saw was laughing.

While this was certainly embarrassing, it wasn't the end of the world for this athlete. He was able to laugh about the experience. A sense of humor will help you do better in cheerleading—as well as in life. Often, being able to laugh at yourself helps you stay focused and motivated. If you take yourself too seriously, you can easily become flustered and make even more mistakes.

Superstitions

Superstitions aren't as common in cheerleading as they are in other sports. Few cheerleaders care about wearing a certain pair of

Cheerleaders perform some difficult stunts that require a lot of practice to perfect. Mistakes are bound to happen—when they do, get up, learn from the mistake and try again!

socks or an item of clothing the way baseball players do—but cheerleading *is* know for the spirit stick, a type of baton used at cheerleading camps. It is awarded not to the squad that is necessarily the best technically but to the one that possesses the best sportsmanship, team spirit, and overall inspiring, positive energy.

Beginning in 1954, the NCA has had the tradition of the spirit stick. It originated as a simple tree limb that was cut, painted, and decorated and given to the winning team. Today, a spirit stick is one of the most symbolic awards a cheerleader can receive. It has long been a superstition that anyone who drops a spirit stick will be cursed along with her team for the remainder of his or her cheering careers.

Superstitions like this may have little foundation in reality—but anything that inspires and builds confidence can be an effective tool for mental preparation for cheerleading.

3
Physical Preparation

Understanding the Words

Your **hamstring** muscles are the group of three muscles at the back of the thigh, which are connected to the knee by the hamstring tendons. Butchers once hung slaughtered pigs by these tendons, hence the name.

Your **groin** is the crease or hollow where the inner part of each thigh joins with the trunk, together with the region around that.

Shin splints are an overuse injury characterized by a dull aching pain brought on by exercise. The pain is felt on either the inside or outside of the shin bone (tibia). The term is applied to several conditions in which either soft tissues or bones are damaged. These conditions include stress fractures of the tibia or fibula, inflammation of the tendons on the outer side of the ankle, increased pressure within muscle compartments, or inflammation of the membrane covering the tibia.

Cross training is participating in different sports in order to get in shape.

Aerobics are exercises that make your muscles require more oxygen, requiring that your heart and lungs work harder.

Because cheerleading is such a physically demanding sport, its participants should take extra precautions before they jump into practice or a competition. Cheerleaders are often required to perform movements such as jumps, splits, and other gymnastics routines. If they are not warmed up properly, these routines could lead to serious injury. In this chapter, a sample of stretches from head to toe is explained to ensure safe performance.

When performing these stretches, keep a few things in mind:

• Each stretch should be held for a minimum of ten seconds. You can increase your flexibility by holding the stretches for longer periods of time—twenty to thirty seconds—and performing them more often.

Proper stretching is an important part of a cheerleader's physical training. Stretching warms muscles, loosens joints, and helps prevent injury.

Fun Facts

- Actress Heather Locklear was ejected from her high school cheerleading squad.
- There are at least 4 million cheerleaders in 81 countries across the globe.
- The top person in a stunt is referred to as the "flyer."
- The most common chant in cheerleading is "GO-FIGHT-WIN!"
- There are seven categories in an official cheerleading competition: individual, partner stunt, and competition cheerleading, mount teams, non-mount teams, and trios.

- Do not bounce or jerk your muscles when you are stretching. This can tear or strain muscles

- Do not rush through your stretches simply to be done with them. This does your body no good and will often lead to injury. Always make sure to take the time to warm up properly.

- Listen to your body and respect its limits. A small amount of discomfort is expected when stretching, but if something causes you excessive pain, stop immediately. Do not compare your stretching ability to anyone else's; everyone has his or her own particular abilities.

Neck Stretches

1. This exercise stretches the neck muscles from side to side. Stand with your legs shoulder-width apart. Tuck your chin into your chest

and hold for ten to twenty seconds. Tilt your right ear toward your right shoulder and hold for ten to twenty seconds. Return to center. Tilt the left ear toward the left shoulder, and again hold for ten to twenty seconds. Repeat three times on each side.

2. This exercise stretches the neck muscles by rotating them gently. Stand with your feet shoulder-width apart. Slowly rotate your head to the right, and look over your right shoulder until you feel a gentle stretch. Hold for ten to twenty seconds. Bring the head to face forward again, and then rotate the neck to the left, looking over the left shoulder until you feel a gentle stretch. Hold for ten to twenty seconds.

The neck rotation (described in neck stretch #1) and the triceps stretch (described in shoulder and arm stretches #2) are illustrated by these diagrams.

Shoulder and Arm Stretches

Cheerleading is a strenuous activity that involves stretching and waving the arms, so you need take time to thoroughly stretch your arms and shoulders.

1. Stand with your feet shoulder-width apart. Clasp your hands behind your back with your elbows fully extended. Then raise your arms as high as you can until you feel a gentle stretch. Hold for ten to twenty seconds.

2. Stand with your feet shoulder-width apart. Raise both arms above your head and bend the left elbow, then grasp it with the right hand. Pull your left upper arm gently toward the middle of your body. You should feel this stretch in your triceps muscle. Hold for ten to twenty seconds.

3. Raise your arms above your head again, then bend the right elbow and grasp it with your left hand. Pull your right upper arm gently toward the middle of your body until you feel a gentle stretch in your triceps. Hold for ten to twenty seconds.

4. Stand with your feet shoulder-width apart. Clasp your hands behind your back, with your elbows fully extended. Lift your arms slightly and bend over at the waist, then lift your arms up even farther, if you can, and hold this stretch for ten to twenty seconds. Repeat two more times.

5. To work both the arms and the waist, stand with your feet shoulder-width apart. Clasp your hands over your head, with your elbows straight. Bend at the waist, and lean to the left until you feel a gentle stretch. Hold for ten to twenty seconds. Return to the starting position, then bend at the waist and lean to the right, again holding for ten to twenty seconds.

Leg and Ankle Stretches

Be sure to take time to properly stretch your legs. It is all too easy for cheer-leaders to pull or strain a muscle—even tear it—by performing high kicks, jumps, or splits before their legs are properly warmed up. Use the following exercises as a guide.

1. This exercise works on your hamstring muscles. Sit on the floor with your legs stretched straight out in front of you. Your feet should be about hip-width apart. Keep your legs as straight as possible, then reach forward and grab hold of either your ankles or toes, depending

The calf stretch shown here can also be done by pushing the arms against a wall, as described in leg and ankle stretch #3.

BETTER PUSH-UPS

To perform effective push-ups, keep your body tight and straight, and lower yourself to the ground. Push yourself back up. Try to do seven to start, and work up until you are doing twenty or more.

on your level of flexibility. Hold for ten to twenty seconds. You should feel this stretch in the backs of the knees and your lower back. Try it with your toes pointing straight up and with your toes pointing forward.

2. This stretch works the groin muscles. Sit on the floor with your knees bent and the soles of your feet pressed together. Hold your feet with your hands, and then rest your elbows on your lower legs. Lean forward and try to touch your forehead to the floor while you press down on your legs. Hold for ten to twenty seconds.

3. To stretch your calves, stand facing a wall and place your hands at about shoulder height. Place one foot in front of the other, keeping the heel of your back foot firmly on the floor. Place your weight on your forward, bent leg, and lean forward, as if you are trying to push against the wall. Hold for ten to twenty seconds. Repeat for the other leg.

4. For the second calf stretch, you need a flight of stairs or a sturdy box. First, line up your heels with the edge of the step. Then move your feet back so that the balls of your feet are on the edge of the step and the rest of our feet are hanging off the edge. (You may need to lean against something or hold on to a railing for balance.) Slowly dip your heels down and then come back up. Repeat ten times.

5. This stretch works your ankles. Stand with your legs shoulder-width apart. Point your right toe so that it is touching the ground, and roll your ankle in a clockwise direction three times. Then roll the ankle counterclockwise three times. Repeat with the left foot.

Cold Muscles

Kansas City Chiefs cheerleading coach Linda Rae Chappell recounts the story of one cheerleader who did not want to take the time to warm up:

At one point, trying out for the cheerleading squad was the most important thing in my life. . . . During each person's tryout time, the rest of us were supposed to be stretching over to the side. . . . Right in the middle of someone's performance, a loud "pop" erupted in the room. It was the sound of my hamstring ripping as I attempted the splits without stretching first . . . the damage was so bad that I was not able to try out. . . . I don't know which muscle hurt the most—my hamstring or my heart.

Push-up diagram showing the proper position of the back, legs and arms during both phases of a push-up.

Special Exercises for Cheerleaders

Since cheerleaders often perform moves that involve jumps, splits, and tumbling, as well as partner stunts or pyramids, here are a few additional exercises you can do to build strength in particular areas.

For a seated hamstring stretch, sit with your legs spread wide apart. Lean over your left leg, and grab hold of the toes of your left foot or left ankle. Point your toes forward and hold for ten to twenty seconds. Sit up. Turn so that you are facing the center, and then lean over your right leg, grabbing hold of the toes of your right foot or ankle. Point your toes forward and hold for ten to twenty seconds. Sit up. Turn so that you are facing the center, and then lean over your right leg, grabbing hold of the toes of your right foot or angle. Point your toes forward and hold for ten to twenty seconds.

The key to being able to perform jumps effectively and without injury is to have a strong abdomen, legs, and arms. You can strengthen these areas by performing the following exercises:

1. The classic push-up exercise develops the strength in your chest muscles, known as the pectorals. Start in a facedown position on the floor. Your back should be level, your toes should be on the floor, and your arms should be locked with your hands shoulder-width apart. To vary this exercise, try moving your arms farther out away from the shoulders (about 6–9 inches/15–23 cm) or closer to the body (about 4 inches/10 cm).

2. This exercise strengthens your abdominal muscles, or "abs." Start in a standing position, feet slightly apart. Jump up into the air, bringing your knees as high as possible to the front of your body. Slap your shins when you have reached the highest point in your jump. Extend your arms into a "T" shape when you land. Repeat this five times, working up to ten repetitions.

3. For another effective abdominal exercise, sit on the floor. Lie down on your back, with your hands either in front of you or behind your head. Your legs should be stretched out straight. Raise your legs at least 2 inches (5 cm) off the floor, with your toes pointed. At the same time, lift your upper body halfway up. You should be looking something like the letter "V." Hold for ten to twenty seconds. Lower your body and legs, but do not let anything touch the floor. Repeat five to ten times.

Don't forget to strengthen your ankles. According to cheerleading coach Linda Rae Chappell, who coached the Kansas City Chiefs football cheerleading team, ankle injuries are the number-one cause of discomfort and loss

Sandra Bullock is one of many famous people who were cheerleaders as teenagers.

SOME MORE FAMOUS CHEERLEADERS

Blake Lively

Kelly Ripa

Reese Witherspoon

Mandy Moore

Sheryl Crow

Cameron Diaz

Eva Longoria

Jessica Simpson

Paul Abdul

Calista Flockhart

Katie Couric

Michael Douglas

Reba McEntire

Sandra Bullock

Halle Berry

of participation time among cheerleaders. She recommends the following exercise to help you strengthen your ankles:

You will need a large exercise band or rubber band (#107, available at most office supply stores). Place the rubber band around both feet at the base of your toes. Keep one foot still, and pull the rubber band outward and upward with the other foot. Keep your heels firmly in place, and hold for ten to twenty seconds. Return to the starting position as slowly as possible, then repeat with the other leg. Repeat this exercise for give to ten minutes a day, working up to twenty minutes.

Wrist-strengthening exercises are also important, because the wrist is used a lot in tumbling moves, as well as in partner stunts (one person balanced on another's shoulders, for example, or cheerleaders balanced in a pyramid formation). The following two exercises work to help develop your wrist muscles.

1. Use a large #107 rubber band or a dumbbell weighing 1–3 pounds (0.5–1.5 kg) Sit in a chair with your knees bent at a 90-degree angle. Hold the rubber band with your palm facing down and with your forearm on your thigh. Secure the opposite end of the rubber band by looping it under your foot. Slowly bend your wrist upward as far as possible. Hold this position for ten seconds, and then lower the wrist slowly, keeping your forearm on your thigh. Repeat ten times.

2. Seated in a chair with your knees bent, position the rubber band as in the previous exercise, with your hand holding the rubber band, your forearm on your thigh, and the opposite end of the rubber band around your foot. This time, your hand should be facing palm-up. Slowly bend the wrist as far as possible, holding for ten seconds, lowering slowly. Repeat ten times.

Cheerleaders need to have supportive, cushioned shoes to help avoid ankle injuries, which are common in cheerleading.

Safety

Cheerleading needs no protective equipment. The best form of protection for cheerleaders is to ensure that all their muscles are properly stretched and warmed up.

That being said, however, everyone associates some pieces of equipment with cheerleaders: megaphones, pompons, and various types of signs, as well as the ever-present cheerleading uniform, which is worn with pride. While none of this equipment offers safety or protection, some thought should be given to the design of the uniform itself, which may help to prevent certain injuries from occurring.

Cheerleading uniforms are often a combination of a sweater, sweatshirt, skirt, vest, top, pants, or shorts. All are in the school/team colors with a logo or design. Many schools have two or even three different types of uniforms. Which uniform is worn depends on several factors, including whether the sport is conducted inside or outside, and what the weather is like. For example, football games, especially in high school and college, are played outdoors and in a season where the weather can be windy, rainy, chilly or cold.

Most cheerleading uniforms for football consist of skirts or pants and a sweater, all in heavy material such as wool or a polyester blend. Sometimes, heavy jackets and gloves are worn if the weather is especially severe.

Basketball games, on the other hand, are played indoors, in a gymnasium that is often warm thanks to all the fans, cheerleaders, and players packed into it. In this case, cheerleading uniforms might consist of a skirt, pants, and a short-sleeved shirt or vest. These items are made out of fabric that is lighter in weight, such as cotton or a rayon blend.

Whatever the case, the most important part of the cheerleader's uniform is her shoes. Always purchase a shoe that provides you with the maximum amount of support and comfort. Remember, ankle injuries are some of the most common injuries sustained by cheerleaders. Canvas or flat-soled shoes (that is, with no shaping at all on the sole) should not be worn because they offer no support for the ankles or arches, which can lead to a twisted ankle, shin splints, or worse.

If you cannot find shoes that are made specifically for cheerleading, which many cheerleading supply or uniform store offer, the next best thing is to find a shoe meant for cross training, aerobics, or running. Take the time to make sure the shoe fits properly. Such shoes can be expensive, but they are well worth the cost. There may be an outlet store in your area that sells well-trusted brand names at discount prices.

One more consideration with regard to shoes is the addition of inserts. These are special pads that go into the shoe, offering additional comfort and support by preventing pressure on a specific part of the foot, or preventing

How to Best Prevent Injuries

- Follow all rules and regulations.
- Practice on mats or pads.
- Wear well-fitting shoes with proper cushion support.
- Require proper spotting.
- Progress **gradually** to difficult stunts and skills.
- Become educated and certified in safety, first aid, and CPR.
- Require and use proper techniques.
- Treat all injuries as soon as they occur.
- Increase flexibility.
- Strengthen lower back, abdomen, and shoulders.
- Increase intensity of practices gradually.

abnormal movement of the foot. They can be purchased in grocery stores, department stores, and specialty shoe stores. Talk to your cheerleading coach or trainer to see if this is something you should consider adding to your shoes.

Because strains, twists, and pulls are common in cheerleading, keep ice, plastic bags, and elastic bandages on hand so that an injury can be treated immediately. Your coach should already have these nearby in case of an emergency, but you can check to see if this has been done or whether you should supply your own.

At times, you may have a limitation that prevents you from fully participating in cheerleading events. In this case, you will probably have to wear a bandage, brace, or some other form of support to keep a muscle or joint as still as possible in order to avoid making it worse or re-injuring it. For example, a cheerleader who has problems with a knee, or who is recovering from a knee injury, may wear a special knee brace and avoid doing certain tumbling moves or jumps so that she does not damage the knee any further. Someone else may wear an ankle brace to support a twisted ankle that is still healing.

These items can be considered a form of safety equipment, and you should wear them exactly as your doctor orders. Do not avoid wearing them just because they make your uniform look "bulky" or don't "go with it." The most important thing is the safety and health of your body, and it is better to put up with a bulky uniform than risk serious injury. After all, you may not only make your injury worse, but you could also cause enough damage that you are not able to participate at all—perhaps even permanently.

4
Common Injuries, Treatment, & Recovery

Understanding the Words

Tendons *are the tough stretchy bands that attach muscles to bones.*

Ligaments *are like tendons, except that they attach bones to other bones.*

Traumatic *has to do with anything that seriously shocks or injures the body.*

Anti-inflammatory *drugs are medicines that help to reduce swelling.*

Cervical *has to do with the neck.*

Your rotator cuff *is the group of muscles holding the shoulder joint in place, which allows you to move your arm in a circle.*

Something that is inflamed *is swollen, red, and hot. Inflammation is the way your body reacts to injury and infection.*

Cartilage *is the tough, rubbery material found in your joints, as well as in your nose and ears.*

Injuries happen in all sports, and cheerleading is no exception. That's why it's so important to take the time to warm up; however, even with proper preparation, injuries can—and do—happen. This chapter will present an overview of some of the most common injuries suffered by cheerleaders. But remember—no book can take the place of a consultation with your coach or doctor!

During sporting events, there are often long periods of time in which cheerleaders are simply standing around, waiting, especially during football games. Keep your muscles warm and stay limber during these times so you do not injure yourself when cheerleading begins again.

According to *The Sports Injury Handbook*, some of the most common injuries cheerleaders suffer are pulled muscles, inflamed **tendons**, and sprained **ligaments**. Hip and groin injuries also happen frequently. Furthermore, certain cheerleading routines, such as pyramids or partner stunts, are more dangerous (for example, one cheerleader standing on the shoulders of another cheerleader, and then performing a gymnastic maneuver off her shoulders). Accidents during these stunts can cause serious head injuries or broken

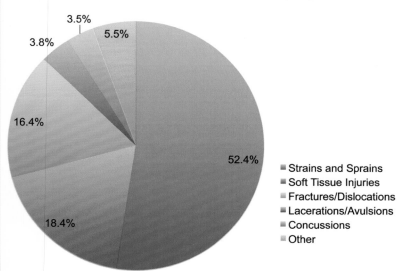

Common Types of Cheerleading Injuries

- 3.5%
- 3.8%
- 5.5%
- 16.4%
- 52.4%
- 18.4%

- Strains and Sprains
- Soft Tissue Injuries
- Fractures/Dislocations
- Lacerations/Avulsions
- Concussions
- Other

As this chart indicates, strains and sprains are the most common cheerleading injuries.

A difficult stunt, like the pyramid shown here, can cause serious injuries if something goes wrong.

necks. Cheerleaders have even died from falling from the upper part of a pyramid. As a result, some schools have banned these high-risk activities.

Head and Neck Injuries

When dealing with injuries to the head and neck, it is better to err on the side of caution. Such injuries are often more serious than you initially think.

CONCUSSION

Concussion is a traumatic injury to the brain, often caused by a violent blow to the head. It may upset your thinking, sight, and balance, and you may even become unconscious.

There are different categories of concussion, depending on how much force was applied to the head and at what angle the head was struck. If the injured person regains consciousness fairly quickly, that is a good sign. Even so, the person should be watched for symptoms such as headache, nausea, or further loss of consciousness, which can indicate bleeding inside the head. If the loss of consciousness lasts for a significant amount of time, or if the person does not recover consciousness at all, the injured person must be taken to a hospital for immediate treatment. Dr. Allan M. Levy, team doctor for the New York Giants, insists that under no circumstances should a person who has suffered

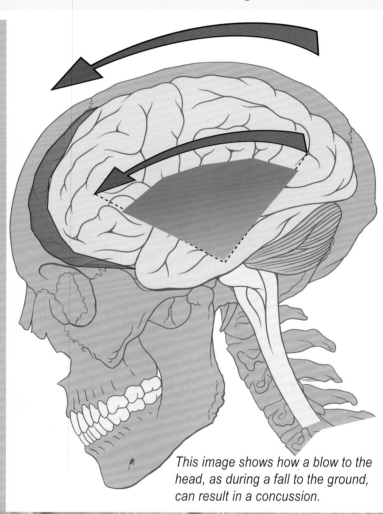

This image shows how a blow to the head, as during a fall to the ground, can result in a concussion.

even a minor concussion be allowed to participate in any physical activity for at least twenty-four hours after the injury.

A concussion is an injury that causes the brain to swell, meaning the skull exerts pressure on the brain. This swelling must be given a chance to go down completely because another blow—even a small one—could cause serious damage to the brain.

WHIPLASH

Sudden, violent movement may strain the muscles and ligaments of the neck, causing whiplash. This can happen if a person is pushed suddenly from behind. Whiplash can be a severe injury, and if you have this kind of injury, you should consult a doctor who can then perform X-rays to make sure that the delicate vertebrae in your neck have not slipped out of alignment or become fractured.

Whiplash is usually treated by two to three days of rest, followed by a period of physical therapy. **Anti-inflammatory** drugs are often prescribed, and some patients also need to wear a **cervical** collar, which is a high collar that supports the weight of the head, thereby taking the strain off the ligaments.

Back Injuries

Back injuries are also common in cheerleading, and usually take the form of a muscle sprain or strain of a ligament. Just because these injuries are common, however, doesn't make them any less serious. One of the most dangerous back injuries is a "slipped" disk in the spine. This happens when the disk that acts as a cushion between two vertebrae bulges out from between the vertebrae, putting pressure on a nerve.

A person without medical training may not be able to tell how serious an injury is, so it is always best to see a doctor when any accidents happen. This is especially true in the case of back injuries, since X-rays and other diagnostic

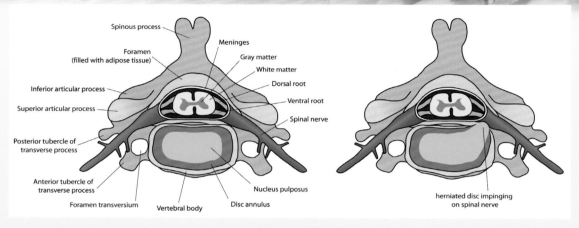

Spinous process
Meninges
Foramen
(filled with adipose tissue)
Gray matter
White matter
Dorsal root
Inferior articular process
Ventral root
Superior articular process
Spinal nerve
Posterior tubercle of
transverse process
Anterior tubercle of
transverse process
Nucleus pulposus
Foramen transversium
Vertebral body
Disc annulus
herniated disc impinging
on spinal nerve

A "slipped" disk in the spine can reduce mobility and cause numbness and pain, especially if the herniated disk hits one of the spinal nerves.

tests may be needed to determine exactly what has happened and what needs to be treated.

For strains and sprains, the typical course of treatment is to keep the patient as still as possible and alternate treating the affected area with a heating pad and ice packs for fifteen to thirty minutes at a time. An anti-inflammatory medication, such as ibuprofen, may be administered. Treatment from a licensed massage therapist may also be helpful.

Shoulder Injuries

The shoulder is unique in that it is a shallow ball-and-socket joint, which makes it more unstable than many other joints. The shoulder is the only joint in the human body that is not held together by its ligaments. The few ligaments that are there only serve to keep it from moving too far in any one direction.

A common shoulder injury experienced by cheerleaders is known as a **rotator cuff** injury. Sports where the arms are constantly brought up over the head, as in cheerleading, can put too much stress on the shoulder joint, and the rotator cuff muscles can stretch out, causing the ball of the joint to become loose inside the shoulder socket. As a result, tendons rub against the bone and become **inflamed** and painful. Most people with a rotator cuff injury report feeling pain in their biceps or deep within their shoulder joint.

Rotator cuff injuries are often mistaken for a strain or tendonitis (inflamed tendons). Doctors will provide medication, such as cortisone injections, to treat inflammation, and the athlete is advised to rest the shoulder. Reducing inflammation will decrease pain, but it will not, however, treat the actual problem—the slippage of the joint—so once the person begins cheering again, the pain will return unless it is given enough time to heal.

After a rotator cuff injury, the muscles in the shoulder need to be strengthened so the ball of the joint will no longer slip out of the socket, which is what causes the pain. Once the slippage stops, the inflammation does as well.

Although surgery is not the preferred method of treatment

Shoulder injuries can occur when the muscles of the rotator cuff are stretched and allow the ball of the humerus, shown in this X-ray, to become loose in its socket.

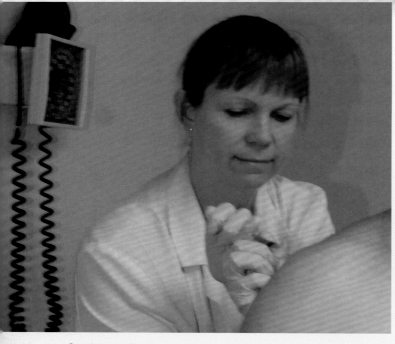

for this injury, a doctor will advise it if a rotator cuff injury is serious enough, or if other treatments have not worked. The surgery will repair the torn tendon. Afterward, the person will need physical therapy and rest from the sport to ensure complete recovery. When surgery is not pre-scribed, physical therapy can often help heal the injury enough to continue with physical activity.

Cortisone shots, usually containing a steroid medication and an anesthetic, are injected in joints to relieve pain and swelling associated with an injury.

Wrist Injuries

Because there are so few muscles in the wrist to be strengthened, most people tend to have weak wrists. Cheerleaders in particular are susceptible to wrist inju-ries because there is so much pressure

Cartwheels, round-offs and handstands are all possible sources of wrist injuries for cheerleaders.

put on them due to the gymnastic aspect of the sport. Cartwheels, round-offs, back handsprings—all these maneuvers put an extraordinary amount of weight on the wrists, causing them to be more vulnerable to accidents.

Treating a sprained wrist typically includes keeping the joint still and rested. Also, be sure to apply ice packs at regular intervals for fifteen to thirty minutes at a time for three to four days. Sometimes, a soft splint is also required to help keep the joint in place while it recovers. To avoid a wrist injury altogether, pay close attention to the wrists during warm-up.

Groin Injuries

The groin muscles, known as the adductor muscles, are located along the inside of the upper thigh. They serve to pull the legs together when they contract and also help to stabilize the hip joints.

Groin injuries are possible when stretching the hip and groin area as in a split. Proper warm-up and stretching is important to prepare the body, and to prevent injury.

A common groin injury suffered by cheerleaders is a groin pull. A pull in a muscle occurs when it has been stretched too far (which can happen when someone attempts a split or a high kick without first properly warming up). Typical symptoms of a groin pull include pain, swelling, bruising, and tenderness, specifically when stretching.

A groin pull is treated in much the same way as any other muscle strain: resting the injury for several days (doctors may recommend at least one week of rest), icing the groin to reduce swelling, and wrapping it with a compression bandage.

Knee Injuries

The knee is a complex joint. It is an intricate network of muscles, tendons, ligaments, cartilage, and bone, which assists us in a variety of motions. It is the most commonly injured joint in the body, accounting for about one-fourth of all sports-related injuries.

Cheerleaders and gymnasts most often suffer from a tear in their anterior cruciate ligaments (A.C.L.), the ligaments on the front of the knee that provide support and stability in the knee joint. An A.C.L. tear is a serious injury and not something that can be treated at home. It most often occurs when the knee is hit by a strong force, in the middle of a twisting motion as you fall, or when someone falls heavily against you.

If the A.C.L. is simply strained, physical therapy alone may repair the tear. However, if the A.C.L. ruptures and tears completely, which is what often happens, surgery is usually needed, followed by extensive physical therapy. A brace may also be worn for some time to give the knee additional support. You may be able to return to your cheerleading activities, but only after a sufficient rest period, under the guidance of your doctor or coach.

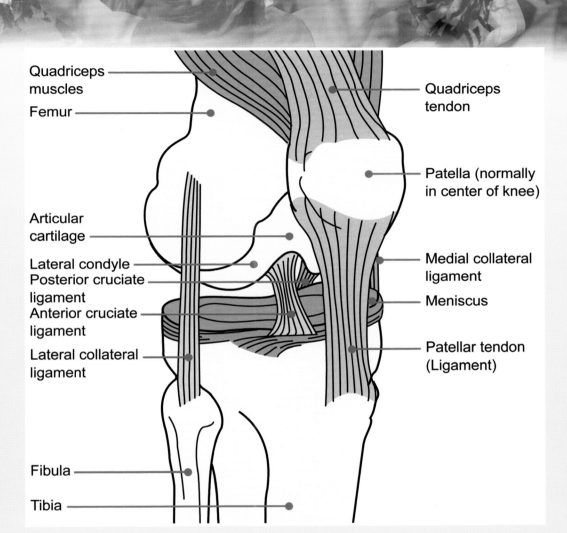

Quadriceps muscles

Femur

Articular cartilage

Lateral condyle

Posterior cruciate ligament

Anterior cruciate ligament

Lateral collateral ligament

Fibula

Tibia

Quadriceps tendon

Patella (normally in center of knee)

Medial collateral ligament

Meniscus

Patellar tendon (Ligament)

The knee joint

Treating Minor Injuries

Cuts

- Grab the cleanest material you can find, such as a wash-cloth or a strip of gauze.
- Cover the cut with the cloth, and apply firm pressure to the wound. Maintain this pressure until the bleeding has stopped.
- Next, clean the wound gently with an antiseptic and spread a thin layer of antibiotic ointment over the wound.
- If you cannot control the bleeding within minutes, seek medical help.

Bruises

- Apply a cold compress or an ice pack to the bruised area as soon as possible. Leave in place for fifteen minutes.

Hamstring Injuries

Hamstring pulls are among the most common muscle pulls and are usually caused by failing to warm up properly. Typical symptoms of a hamstring pull can include sharp pain and swelling, and, in the most severe tears, bruising due to internal bleeding within the muscle. You may also be unable to raise

Repeat several times a day to alleviate the pain and prevent swelling.

Sprains

- Immediately immerse the sprained area in ice water, or apply an ice pack for twenty minutes to control the swelling. Repeat in twenty-minute intervals over a period of at least four hours until the swelling has stopped.
- Elevate the sprained limb to at least waist level to help alleviate swelling.
- Once the swelling has stopped, soak the sprained area three times a day—first in warm water for twenty minutes, then in icy water for twenty minutes.

your leg straight off the ground more than a short distance without feeling pain. Typical treatment includes rest, ice, and compression: usually resting for at least two or three days; icing the muscle for twenty minutes, three to four times a day; and wrapping the muscle in a compression bandage.

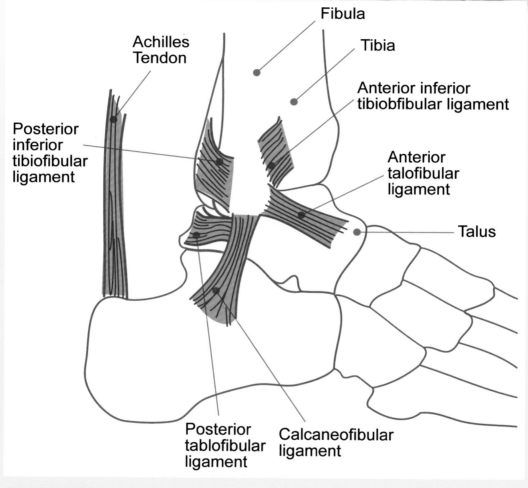

The ankle joint

Ankle Injuries

According to cheerleading coach Linda Rae Chappell, ankle injuries are the most common injury suffered by cheerleaders. Ankles are sprained when the ligaments are stretched too far and tear. When treating an ankle sprain, a doctor may recommend that you keep the foot rested for a least the first twenty-four hours, placing no weight on the ankle if at all possible (which may mean you have to use crutches). An ankle sprain is often accompanied by a great deal of swelling, so you may be told to ice the ankle for twenty minutes, remove the ice for twenty minutes, ice it again, and so on, for at least the first forty-eight hours, or until the ankle returns to normal size. You may also be advised to wrap the ankle with a compression bandage and keep it elevated higher than your heart by propping it up on pillows at night in order to reduce swelling and bruising. Typically, after a couple of days, you may be able to put weight on the ankle again.

5
Nutrition and Supplements

Understanding the Words

A **nutritionist** is someone who specializes in helping people eat healthy diets.

A **regimen** is a systematic plan.

Moderation means in the middle—not too much, not too little.

Synthesis means the process of putting something together.

Something that is **fortified** is made stronger than it would have been otherwise.

Although practice and training are an important part of being safe and successful in cheerleading, you also need to think about what you take into your body. All athletes, including cheerleaders, must be careful to eat a proper blend of nutrients to make sure their bodies and minds perform as well as they possibly can. This doesn't just mean eating healthy foods, but also choosing when to eat, how much to eat, and whether to take dietary supplements. Of course, when you choose a new diet or supplements, you should consult with a **nutritionist**, doctor, or some other expert. Don't make up your own nutritional program!

What to Eat

While a balanced diet is important for everyone, it is even more important for athletes. Typically, an athlete has to eat considerably more than other people do. The United States Food and Drug

	Calorie Range		
Children	**Sedentary** →		**Active**
2–3 years	1,000	→	1,400
Females			
4–8 years	1,200	→	1,800
9–13	1,600	→	2,200
14–18	1,800	→	2,400
19–30	2,000	→	2,400
31–50	1,800	→	2,200
51+	1,600	→	2,200
Males			
4–8 years	1,400	→	2,000
9–13	1,800	→	2,600
14–18	2,200	→	3,200
19–30	2,400	→	3,000
31–50	2,200	→	3,000
51+	2,000	→	2,800

Daily caloric needs vary depending on age, body size and activity level. Athletes typically need to eat more calories in order to sustain an active lifestyle.

MyPyramid at www.mypyramid.gov gives useful information about diet, exercise and daily calorie needs.

Administration (FDA) suggests that the average American should eat about 2000 calories a day. But because cheerleading is so physically demanding, you must be sure to have enough energy to practice and perform. Don't skimp on nutrition, thinking that doing so will keep you slim; an audience or judges will not be impressed or inspired by sluggish, lifeless movements—and your body needs the right fuel to have the energy and strength it needs.

Cheerleaders often feel pressured to stay thin—or become thinner. Remember that everyone has a unique body, which comes with its own unique healthy weight; someone who is curvier may very well be healthier than someone who is very thin and restricts her diet. What is most important is to eat healthy foods from a variety of food groups, and get lots of exercise. If you do this, you are sure to have your own best body.

Good nutrition is made up of a variety of elements, including carbohydrates, protein, fats, minerals, and vitamins.

CARBOHYDRATES

Carbs are foods rich in a chemical called starch, which is what the body breaks down to get energy. Starchy foods include breads and grains, veg-

This bottom portion of the pyramid on page 71 contains suggestions on how to lead a healthy lifestyle.

GRAINS Make half your grains whole	VEGETABLES Vary your veggies	FRUITS Focus on fruits	MILK Get your calcium-rich foods	MEAT & BEANS Go lean with protein
Eat at least 3 oz. of whole-grain cereals, breads, crackers, rice, or pasta every day 1 oz. is about 1 slice of bread, about 1 cup of breakfast cereal, or ½ cup of cooked rice, cereal, or pasta	Eat more dark-green veggies like broccoli, spinach, and other dark leafy greens Eat more orange vegetables like carrots and sweetpotatoes Eat more dry beans and peas like pinto beans, kidney beans, and lentils	Eat a variety of fruit Choose fresh, frozen, canned, or dried fruit Go easy on fruit juices	Go low-fat or fat-free when you choose milk, yogurt, and other milk products If you don't or can't consume milk, choose lactose-free products or other calcium sources such as fortified foods and beverages	Choose low-fat or lean meats and poultry Bake it, broil it, or grill it Vary your protein routine — choose more fish, beans, peas, nuts, and seeds
For a 2,000-calorie diet, you need the amounts below from each food group. To find the amounts that are right for you, go to MyPyramid.gov.				
Eat 6 oz. every day	Eat 2½ cups every day	Eat 2 cups every day	Get 3 cups every day; for kids aged 2 to 8, it's 2	Eat 5½ oz. every day

Find your balance between food and physical activity
- Be sure to stay within your daily calorie needs.
- Be physically active for at least 30 minutes most days of the week.
- About 60 minutes a day of physical activity may be needed to prevent weight gain.
- For sustaining weight loss, at least 60 to 90 minutes a day of physical activity may be required.
- Children and teenagers should be physically active for 60 minutes every day, or most days.

Know the limits on fats, sugars, and salt (sodium)
- Make most of your fat sources from fish, nuts, and vegetable oils.
- Limit solid fats like butter, margarine, shortening, and lard, as well as foods that contain these.
- Check the Nutrition Facts label to keep saturated fats, *trans* fats, and sodium low.
- Choose food and beverages low in added sugars. Added sugars contribute calories with few, if any, nutrients.

Food	Milligrams of Calcium
Yogurt, fat-free plain (1 cup)	452
Soy beverage with added calcium (1 cup)	368
Orange juice with added calcium (1 cup)	351
Fruit yogurt, low-fat (1 cup)	345
Cheese (e.g., low-fat or fat-free American, 2 oz., about 3 slices)	323
Milk, fat-free (1 cup)	306
Milk, 1% low-fat (1 cup)	290
Tofu, firm, with added calcium sulfate (1/2 cup)	253
Cheese pizza (1 slice)*	182
Bok choy, boiled (1 cup)	158
Spinach, cooked from frozen (1 cup)**	146
Soybeans, cooked (1 cup)	130
Frozen yogurt, soft-serve vanilla (1/2 cup)	103
Macaroni and cheese (1 cup)*	92
Almonds (1 oz.)	70
Broccoli, cooked (1 cup, chopped)	62
Tortillas, flour (7")	58
Broccoli, raw (1 cup, chopped)	43
Tortillas, corn (6")	42

*This chart shows some foods that are good sources of calcium. *These foods are high in fat and/or sodium and should be eaten less often. **Calcium from this food may not be as well absorbed as from some other greens.*

etables such as potatoes, cereal, pasta, and rice. Roughly half an athlete's calories should come from carbohydrates, but you should beware of heavily processed carbohydrates such as sugary foods and white bread made with bleached flour. These foods are quickly broken down into sugars, which the body processes into fats if it does not immediately burn them off. The best carbohydrate choices for an athlete are pasta and whole-grain foods, as well

Cholesterol

A lot of bad things have been said about cholesterol—but most of this bad press is focused on LDLs, or low-density lipoproteins, which are a kind of cholesterol that can clog our blood vessels and make our hearts work harder. Our bodies make this cholesterol out of saturated fats, such as those found in animal fat from meats, butter, and whole milk. However, there is a kind of cholesterol known as HDLs, or high-density lipoproteins, which have a good effect on the body. Increasing your HDL levels can be as easy as exercising regularly.

as starchy vegetables, which contain vitamins as well as carbohydrates. A balanced diet avoids the "empty calories" supplied by white bread and sugars.

PROTEIN

Proteins are important chemicals found in all living things; these chemicals are used to perform specific functions inside our body's cells. Each protein is a long, folded, chain-like molecule made up of "links" called amino acids. Our bodies can break down proteins that are found in foods into their base amino acids and use them to build new proteins that make up our muscles and bones. For this reason, during any exercise regimen, it is important to eat enough protein to give your body the building blocks it needs to become stronger. The best sources of proteins are meats and dairy products (such as milk or cheese), as well as eggs and certain vegetables (such as soy, beans, and rice).

A good rule of thumb for how much protein to eat is that the number of grams should be equal to about one-third of your body weight in pounds. For example, a 200-pound person should eat at least 60 or 70 grams of protein every day, or a 120-pound person should have roughly 40 grams of protein.

FATS

Lots of times, we think of fats as bad for us, since eating too much of them is unhealthy. However, fat is an important ingredient needed to make our bodies work correctly. Without fats, our bodies cannot absorb certain vitamins as well. Also, our skin and hair need some amount of fat to grow correctly. However, fats should still be eaten in **moderation**—no more than 70 grams a day. The best sources of fat are

Eating a wide variety of fruits and vegetables as part of a healthy diet is an ideal way to get many essential vitamins and minerals.

vegetable oils, olive oil, and nuts. Many foods contain saturated fats, which lead to the formation of cholesterol and can force your heart to work harder.

MINERALS AND VITAMINS

We all need to eat plenty of fruit and vegetables to get the vitamins we need. And while all the major minerals are good for athletes, cheerleaders should make sure to consume two minerals in particular: calcium and iron. These two are also some of the minerals most likely to be under-consumed by a young athlete.

DID YOU KNOW?
Although vitamin C will help you absorb both iron and calcium better, if you eat calcium and iron together, they will interfere with your body's ability to absorb each of them.

Calcium is important to strengthen bones. It is especially needed for younger athletes whose bones are still developing. Unfortunately, the body often absorbs calcium poorly; usually, only 20 percent of the calcium in a diet is consumed from the original food. Drinking lots of milk with calcium-rich cereal is best. Cheese is also an easy source to include as a snack or in a sandwich. Eating foods that contain vitamin C will also help you absorb calcium better.

Iron is another mineral needed to keep a gymnast healthy. Red meat and fish, as well as tofu and black-eyed peas, are all foods that are heavy in iron. Eating foods that are rich in vitamin C along with foods that contain iron will also help your body absorb iron better.

Dietary Supplements

Many athletes seek to improve their performance by taking dietary supplements, which are pills or drinks that contain nutrients or chemicals to improve their physical health or performance. Dietary supplements do not include illegal performance enhancing drugs. Instead, they contain vitamins and minerals, or chemicals that help the body use vitamins more efficiently. Although when properly used, supplements can improve overall heath and performance, you should always consult a doctor or another health expert before taking them. Some examples of common supplements include vitamin tablets, creatine, and protein shakes or powder.

VITAMIN TABLETS

For many reasons, we do not always get the vitamins and nutrients we need. Often, this is because our diets are

Red meat is the most familiar source of iron, but there are many other foods that contain higher amounts of iron.

Food	Iron (mg/serving)
Fortified cereal, 1 cup	5-30
Clams, canned, ¼ cup	11
Liverwurst, 2 oz	6
Baked beans, canned, 1 cup	4
Beef burrito, 1	3
Lean sirloin, broiled, 3 oz	3
Wheat germ, ¼ cup	3
Prune juice, ¾ cup	2
Bean burrito, 1	2
Beef, lean ground, cooked, 3 oz	2
White rice, enriched, ½ cup	1

mg = milligrams
oz = ounces

not as balanced as they should be. Sometimes, it is because the foods that are available to us have been processed in such a way that they lose nutrients. Also, exhausted soil all over the country means that fruits and vegetables are often not as nutrient-rich as they should be. In many cases, we can get the vitamins we need from vitamin supplements. These supplements, which are usually taken as a pill, sometimes contain a balanced mixture of vitamins and nutrients (known as a multivitamin), and sometimes they contain a single vitamin or mineral that our diet is lacking. It is possible to overdose on certain vitamins, however, so be careful when taking vitamin supplements. Don't assume that because a little of something is good for you that a lot of it will be better! Vitamins and minerals don't work that way. And always talk to your doctor before beginning to take supplements of any kind.

CREATINE

Creatine is a specific protein that is naturally found in your body's muscle cells. When taken in larger doses than is found in the body, creatine has the effect of increasing the rate of protein synthesis within your body cells. What this means is that you will have more energy to exercise, and you will see a greater improvement in strength and speed when you do exercise. However, putting any chemical into your body can have negative effects as well, and you should talk to a doctor before beginning to take creatine. What's more, creatine is only suitable for adult athletes, so young people (those under the age of 17) should not take it.

PROTEIN SUPPLEMENTS

Getting enough protein from the food you eat can be difficult. Eating protein immediately after a workout is recommended (in order to refuel your body), but most people don't feel up to cooking or preparing themselves a meal

FOOD	AMOUNT	PROTEIN IN GRAIN
Chicken	3 oz.	20
Ground beef	3 oz.	21
Pork chop, lean	2 oz.	15
Mil,	1 cup	9
Egg	1	6
Cheddar cheese	1 oz.	7
Beans	3/4 cup	11
Peanut butter	2 Tbsp.	8
Bread	1 slice	2
Cooked cereal	½ cup	2
Dry cereal	1 oz.	1-4
Rice	½ cup	5
Nuts	2 Tbsp.	5
Soybeans	½ cup	10
Cooked vegetables	½ cup	1-2

Protein shakes should be used only occasionally as a supplement. The bulk of an athlete's protein should come from a balanced diet.

Staying Hydrated

The best diet in the world is no good if you become dehydrated. Dehydration occurs when your body doesn't have enough water, leading to fatigue, dizziness, and headaches, all of which can hurt your performance when cheerleading. It's best to carry a bottle of water with you for the whole day before a practice or game to make sure that you are fully hydrated. In addition, you should be drinking water throughout the game to avoid becoming dehydrated as you sweat. Staying fully hydrated has many benefits besides helping your performance in the game—it can help mental concentration, improve digestive health, and reduce the risk of kidney stones.

immediately after a workout. That's why protein shakes are often a convenient choice. Many shakes contain blends of protein, carbohydrates, and fats, and some include vitamins, to help balance an athlete's diet. Furthermore, having protein immediately after a workout can help repair the damage sustained by your muscles during the workout. However, you should remember that while protein shakes are useful for supplementing your diet, they should not be used to replace normal food in any significant quantities. You can get plenty of nutrients from a balanced diet that cannot be replaced by artificial protein shakes, regardless of how **fortified** they may be. A nutritionist can tell you how to fit protein or supplement shakes into your diet safely and effectively.

Basic Nutritional Guidelines

Good nutrition is essential to good cheerleading. Here are a few guidelines to follow:

- Eat foods packed with nutrients. Keep junk and processed foods to a minimum. These contain calories that the body does not use optimally because of their low vitamin and mineral content.

- Drink one liter of water per 1000 calories of food consumed.

- Eat a diet that contains a variety of foods, such as breads and cereals, fruits, vegetables, meat and meat substitutes, and dairy.

- Use meal replacement shakes, fruit smoothies, or bars only when necessary. Always keep bars available in places such as a book bag, a purse, glove compartment, or locker for those times when poor nutrition might be the alternative, such as a busy day at a competition or while traveling.

- Take a multivitamin and mineral supplement daily, but be careful not to overdo it, especially when taking other supplements as well (such as meal-replacements, bars, or shakes). Follow the directions, and never take more than the recommended dosage.

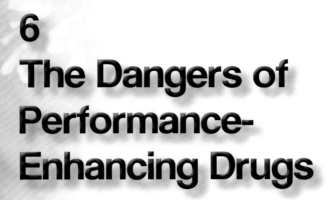

6
The Dangers of Performance-Enhancing Drugs

Understanding the Words

To **stimulate** *means to encourage something to happen.*

An **electrolyte** *organizes the electrically charged particles that are in body fluids such as blood.*

Your **metabolism** *consists of all the processes that are constantly going on within your body.*

Stigma *is a feeling or mark of shame in society.*

If you follow sports, you have most likely heard of athletes using steroids and other drugs to improve their performance—and while you may think of baseball or football when it comes to performance-enhancing drugs, cheerleading is sometimes involved, as well.

Steroids

The most common performance enhancers are anabolic steroids. These chemicals are similar to testosterone, which is the male hormone naturally produced by the body to help stimulate muscle growth. That's why when a player takes anabolic steroids, he receives a boost to his speed and strength that is greater than what the body could normally produce on its own. Male cheerleaders, who form the bases for stunts, need to be very strong gymnasts; they often feel pressured to be extremely muscular. As a result, the use of anabolic steroids has become more and more common in the sport. Athletes often use steroids—which are only legal by prescription from a doctor for certain illnesses—to increase their strength (through muscle mass) and produce temporary weight gain.

Steroid use has become common enough that it may not seem all that serious—but it has serious health consequences, and it can get you kicked off your squad. Most college squads conduct drug testing of each athlete before or during the season.

Anabolic Steroid Use by Students 2008 Monitoring the Future Survey			
	8th Grade	**10th Grade**	**12th Grade**
Lifetime††	1.4%	1.4%	2.2%
Past Year	0.9%	0.9%	1.5%
Past Month	0.5%	0.5%	1.0%

The Monitoring the Future Survey is used annually by the National Institute on Drug Abuse (NIDA) to assess drug use among 8th, 10th and 12th grade students in the United States.

Steroids can cause an unhealthy increase in cholesterol levels and an increase in blood pressure. This stresses the heart, and leads to an increased risk of heart disease. Large doses of steroids can also lead to liver failure, and they have a negative effect on blood sugar levels, sometimes causing problems similar to diabetes.

If an adolescent (typically someone under the age of about seventeen) takes anabolic steroids, the risks are often much worse. Steroids stop bones from growing, which results in stunted growth. In addition, the risks to the liver and heart are much greater, since a young person's liver and heart are not fully

Cheerleaders who are going to be lifted, carried, or thrown into the air try to keep as fit and as light as possible.

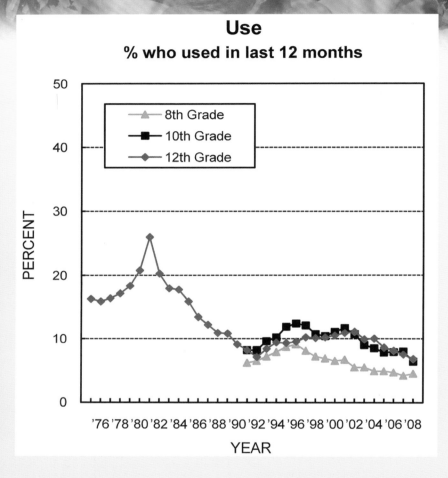

Use

% who used in last 12 months

The use of amphetamines among teenagers has been declining steadily over the past decade as the perceived risks of using have increased.

matured and are more susceptible to the damage that steroids can cause. Furthermore, taking steroids puts you at a greater risk of psychological problems that generally begin with aggression but often lead to much more serious issues. Considering these health risks, as well as the fact that anabolic steroids are almost universally banned from organized sports, they should not be used, except by those who have legitimate medical conditions that require their use.

Amphetamines

Amphetamines are more commonly known as speed. They increase the heart rate and the body's entire metabolism, like a bolt of electricity that revs an engine. Amphetamines charge the body and mind and put them into over-drive. Female cheerleaders most often abuse amphetamines in order to lose weight, but the drug also increases an athlete's energy level, allowing her to exercise longer and harder.

The use of amphetamine during strenuous physical activity can be extremely dangerous, however, especially when combined with alcohol; some athletes have died as a result. The drug's side effects include decreased appetite, insomnia, numbness, and heart problems, including heart attack.

Diuretics

Female cheerleaders, especially "flyers," will go to extreme lengths to main-tain a certain weight limit—one that is often set by the coach or team rules. Diuretics drain the body of liquids, which makes you weigh less. One of the most commonly abused diuretics is called furosemide. This drug can be used to shed water weight, and it is also used as a masking agent to hide other banned substances in an athlete's blood stream.

Many risks are associated with using diuretics. The fluid loss involved in diuretic abuse can result in diminished heart output, which reduces your abil-ity to breathe and can hinder athletic performance. Also, as more fluids are lost, the body's ability to circulate blood to the skin and moderate body heat is often impaired. Other side effects include muscle cramping, exhaustion, and even cardiac arrest. Some athletes have died because of a loss of electro-lytes from abusing diuretics. It is best to try and maintain a healthy, realistic weight through exercise and a healthy diet.

Cheering Lingo

Attack the Crowd: A technique used to get the audience involved in a cheer, dance, or song. This might mean cheering with a bit more enthusiasm or including the audience themselves in a chant.

Base: This is the cheerleader who stays on the ground or floor while lifting the flyer into a stunt. A base is the person on the bottom of a stunt or pyramid.

Arabesque: One leg is down straight and the other leg is behind you almost at a ninety-degree angle to your back.

Basket toss: a stunt usually using three or more bases who toss the flyer into the air. Two of the bases have interlocked their hands. In the air the flyer may do any jump before returning to the cradle.

Getting Caught

The price of getting caught taking any of these illegal performance-enhancing drugs is very high. When an athlete achieves national or international status, and then officials catch him using performance-enhancing drugs, the results can be as dramatic the loss of a medal. Drugs take away the pride of accomplishment and replace it with the stigma of being considered a cheater. Getting caught taking drugs can ruin careers that took years to build. On top of that, taking drugs is dangerous. It's simply not worth it!

Buckets: when a cheerleader holds his or her arms straight out in front, with their firsts facing down as if they were holding the handle of a bucket in each hand.

Candle sticks: a cheer motion where a cheerleader extends his or her arms out in front with fists facing each other as if they were holding a lit candle in each hand.

Cradle catch: an end movement where a base catches a flyer after tossing her into the air. The base holds the flyer under her thighs and around her back.

Deadman: when the flyer falls backward or forward out of a stunt. Three or four people catch the flyer and could possibly push the flyer back up to the bases' hands.

Flyer: The person that is elevated into the air by the bases; the person that is on top of a pyramid/stunt.

Cheerleading is all about inspiring others, both players and spectators. Doing that takes a certain kind of personality, as well as athletic skill. According to one cheerleader, "A good cheerleader is not measured by the height of her jumps but by the span of her spirit." You can build that spirit by preparing, mentally and physically; by dealing with injuries; by eating good nutrition—and by staying away from performance-enhancing drugs.

And as another cheerleader said, "Simply because we do not run across goal lines, slam dunk basketballs, or hit home runs, doesn't mean we can't change the score."

Further Reading

Beim, Gloria and Ruth Winter. *The Female Athlete's Body Book : How to Prevent and Treat Sports Injuries in Women and Girls*. New York, NY: McGraw-Hill, 2003.

Carrier, Justin and Donna McKay. *Complete Cheerleading*. Champaign, Ill: Human Kinetics, 2005.

de Alba, Miriam Lopez Hernandez. *Cheerleading: Technique-Training-Show*. Aachen, Germany: Meyer & Meyer Fachverlag und Buchhandel GmbH, 2009.

Parton, K. *Coaching Cheerleading: Building A Successful Program*. Spindale, NC: Deep Creek Publishing, Ltd, 2009.

Price, Robert. *The Ultimate Guide to Weight Training for Cheerleading*. Sportsworkout.com, 2007.

Wilson, Leslie. *The Ultimate Guide to Cheerleading: For Cheerleaders and Coaches*. Roseville, California: Prima Publishing, 2003.

Find Out More on the Internet

Kids Sports Network
"Cheerleading Coaching Resources"
www.ksnusa.org/cheerlinks.htm

National Cheer Safety Foundation
www.nationalcheersafety.com

Sports Injury Clinic
www.sportsinjuryclinic.net

Varsity
www.varsity.com

Disclaimer

The websites listed on this page were active at the time of publication. The publisher is not responsible for websites that have changed their address or discontinued operation since the date of publication. The publisher will review and update the websites upon each reprint.

Bibliography

About.com, "Cheerleading," cheerleading.about.com/od/coachingcheerleading/a/safety.htm (15 February 2010).

About.com, "Orthopedics," orthopedics.about.com/od/rotatorcuff/tp/rotator-cuff.htm, (17 February 2010).

Ask the Dietician, "Sports Nutrition," www.dietitian.com/sportnut.html (22 February 2010).

Flyertalk, "Cheerleading Injuries More Than Double," www.flyertalk.com/forum/omni/510163-cheerleading-injuries-more-than-double.html (15 February 2010).

Frandsen, Betty Rae, Kathryn J. Frandsen and Kent P. Frandsen. *Where's Mom Now That I Need Her?* Sandy, UT: Aspen West Publishing Company, 2004.

Fun Trivia, "Cheerleading," www.funtrivia.com/en/Sports/Cheerleading-711.html (15 February 2010).

Hyperstrike, "Nutrition for Cheerleading," www.hyperstrike.com/Nutrition-For-Cheerleading-Part-1-Article-40.aspx (22 February 2010).

KidzWorld, "Cheerleading Tips and Terms," www.kidzworld.com/article/4906-cheerleading-tips-and-terms (22 February 2010).

ThinkExist, "Quotations," en.thinkexist.com/search/searchQuotation. asp?search=cheerleading (15 February 2010).

Varsity, "2009 NCA/NDA Collegiate Cheer and Dance Championship," varsity.com/event.aspx?event=1144 (17 February 2010).

Index

Picture Credits

Creative Commons Attribution Generic/Attribution ShareAlike/Unported 3.0
army.arch: pg. 11
George, Angela: pg. 46
hr.icio: pg. 16
keps1230: pg. 34
lifeabundantly: pg. 55
Lynch, Patrick: pg. 56
mcmorgan08: pg. 59
Monica's Dad: pg. 38, 48, 86
robertpaulyong: pg. 62
Sandstein: pg. 79
terren in Virginia: pg. 33
uwdigitalcollections: pg. 12
Vironaveah: pg. 61

GNU Free Documentation License, Version 1.2
Vidralta: pg. 40

United States Air Force
Reddick, Adriane: pg. 20

United States Marine Corps
Shields, Lance Cpl. Shelby R.: pg. 23

United States Navy
Reckard, Bryan: pg. 28

About the Author and the Consultants

Gabrielle Vanderhoof is a former competitive figure skater. She now works in publishing and public relations. This is her first time writing for Mason Crest.

Susan Saliba, Ph.D., is a senior associate athletic trainer and a clinical instructor at the University of Virginia in Charlottesville, Virginia. A certified athletic trainer and licensed physical therapist, Dr. Saliba provides sports medicine care, including prevention, treatment, and rehabilitation for the varsity athletes at the university. Dr. Saliba is a member of the national Athletic Trainers' Association Educational Executive Committee and its Clinical Education Committee.

Eric Small, M.D., a Harvard-trained sports medicine physician, is a nationally recognized expert in the field of sports injuries, nutritional supplements, and weight management programs. He is author of *Kids & Sports* (2002) and is Assistant Clinical professor of pediatrics, Orthopedics, and Rehabilitation Medicine at Mount Sinai School of Medicine in New York. He is also Director of the Sports Medicine Center for Young Athletes at Blythedale Children's Hospital in Valhalla, New York. Dr. Small has served on the American Academy of Pediatrics Committee on Sports Medicine, where he develops national policy regarding children's medical issues and sports.